# Soul
# Mouth

## Marilyn Bowering

EXILE
editions

Library and Archives Canada Cataloguing in Publication

Bowering, Marilyn, 1949-
    Soul mouth / Marilyn Bowering.

Poems.
ISBN 978-1-55096-300-7

    I. Title.

PS8553.O9S68 2012      C811'.54      C2012-906210-3

Design and Composition by Hourglass Angels~mc
Typeset in Fairfield and Stone fonts at the Moons of Jupiter Studios
Cover Painting by Maya Bowering
Printed by Imprimerie Gauvin

Published by Exile Editions Ltd ~ www.ExileEditions.com
144483 Southgate Road 14 – GD, Holstein ON, N0G 2A0
Printed and Bound in Canada; Publication Copyright © Exile Editions, 2012

The publisher would like to acknowledge the financial support of the Canada
Council for the Arts, the Government of Canada through the Canada Book
Fund (CBF), the Ontario Arts Council, and the Ontario Media Development
Corporation, for our publishing activities.

 **Conseil des Arts** **Canada Council**
du Canada          for the Arts

**ONTARIO ARTS COUNCIL**
**CONSEIL DES ARTS DE L'ONTARIO**

Canadian Sales: The Canadian Manda Group, 165 Dufferin Street,
Toronto ON  M6K 3H6    www.mandagroup.com    416 516 0911

North American and International Distribution, and U.S. Sales:
Independent Publishers Group, 814 North Franklin Street,
Chicago IL  60610    www.ipgbook.com    toll free: 1 800 888 4741

# Soul
# Mouth

For Xan

*Originally, you were clay.*
*From being mineral, you became vegetable.*
*From vegetable, you became animal, and from animal, man...*
*And you have to go through a hundred different worlds yet.*

—RUMI

*Let the honey accumulate in the comb*
*Let it not leak or drizzle away*
*Let the bear's paw not encounter it*
*Let the bear's snout not enter it*

—P.K. PAGE

*See also, then, men carrying past the wall implements of all*
*kinds that rise above the wall, and human images and shapes of*
*animals as well, wrought in stone and wood and every material...*
*A strange image you speak of, he said, and strange prisoners.*
*Like to us, I said.*

—PLATO

# Contents

## BODY

## Soul

## THE STORYTELLERS ON THEIR CARPETS

# BODY

# Starting School

After you have wiped off flies,
eaten the jelly of strength and cunning,
taken the knob of cheese and the quivering bird,
and left home with these in your pocket,

and you've met the giant,
given blood from a stone,
thrown the stone without return,
stripped the cherry tree of sweetness—

someone whispers: Every cause
has a pearl; every cure has effect,
but who will protect the innocent?

You are walking home from school;
a classmate stalks you.
He has five stones in his pocket.
He lets fly the first and the second
and the third. You run so fast that the fourth and fifth
remain in the air: they do not fall to earth.

Then your mother says: That boy in your class, the one
who followed you home, his sister strangled to death in her crib
on a strand of real pearls. Imagine.

# Seine

I was born by the Seine River:
it rolled slowly,
it spilled and soaked the grasses,
many birds traversed it,
the river bank was forbidden
though aprons from the nearby houses
fluted the air like river gulls.

There were small boats stashed, and a pigpen in the yard;
my brother rinsed underwear outdoors in a tub
while great uncles mended nets under the stairs.
I remember stepping from the window into water:
the house was a living island, its raincoat flying,
boots to its knees, a peddler's sack of poison.
It wrenched loose on restless foundations,
edged close to the riverbank and an episode
of drowned children.
When a stranger arrived, carrying chickens,
he took off his coat, and hung it, headless,
on the clothesline.

I was born by the Seine River:
it rolled slowly,
it spilled and soaked the grasses;
the river bank was forbidden,
many birds traversed it,
I was among them.

# Crow

*Twa craws* fly over my head in the winter sunshine;
it doesn't mean anything.
Crows at the beach, bead eyes scrolling,
crows flitting down from the fir tree
bent over the garden—

martyr crows,
crows with the gift of derision—

in that time of loneliness,
the apples binned, the rain soaked cabbages—
crows in the boughs screeching, *Yes!*

They couldn't see me, but I could see them—
I had to row over their water green eyelids
to get to the other side.

# Breakdown

The truck was blue,
coal sacks swagged
against its sides,
snow fell on our tongues,
the pickup slewed,
the smoke-thick skies burned cold;
and near where we stopped, men and boys
hung fishing lines over the wet bridge railing.

We climbed out of the truck bed, ears stinging,
to buy ice cream cones from the shop.
Our father unfolded his wallet,
our mother stayed in the cab,
her face turned to the rear window.
She cleared a path with her glove
to view the herring below the bridge.

When we returned,
she said she'd forgotten her wedding dress
and photographs in a shed
while escaping the flood:
there was no way, now, to prove
what she'd been,
who she was.

# Fish

The tug on the line was a stocking snag,
the tuck of a blanket at night while I slept,
the flash of a dream, leaf-sweet in daylight;
the water was sunlit and razor-edged.

There's nothing there, my brother said.
It's lake-weed, he said.
But our father tried the line and said:
Wind it in slowly.

The squint of my eyes, the gaff nearby—
my arms were sore and the reel too shrill—
the fish flipped up like a small cache of silver,
then we watched it lie still.

Let it go, my father said.
But my hands were raw,
and all over the world
there were wide pink mouths
that could never be filled.

# Naked

Ahem, we've work to do:
unbutton that blouse, release the waistband—those shoes—
slip-ons are better, they slip off.
Why have laces at all?
Now that you're naked, forget the cold:
it's only the north wind on the breath of your childhood,
hours at a window, fingernails tracing
intricate cells of frost.

You called to your father to hurry;
you twisted and squirmed on the skating shack bench
while he laced your skates.
The men kept the heat in the stove in a roar,
the girls dressed loudly, the boys with mittened hands
in their armpits.
You tottered away from the frozen shore,
towed by your father. The wind nipped tucks of hair
free of your hat and whispered:

One day the planet
will ask you to tell a story in return for today.
Not everyone gets to fly
without frostbite in exceptionally low temperatures,
under a kind gaze,
and believe it is good to be born
without clothes.

# Banff, 1953

A two-tone Chevrolet,
a handle-strap to hold me to the window glass:
we crossed the brown and frost of April,
the horses heavy-maned,
and swans just landing on the lake.
Back in the prairie dust,
an aunt and uncle in a barrack's shack.
Inside, too, the bunk beds where we'd slept,
my nurse's kit, with candy pills, parked on a blanket.

My uncle and my dad were meat-fed men,
my aunt and mother slim,
their faces smooth with pleasure—
chatelaines.
Each had a pocketbook
she carried when she shopped,
its contents closed as lives
of voles in pastureland
by which we drove that spring.

The mountains still ahead of us were new—
we looked to them—
rough sketches in an untried hand,
they might be friends.

# Museum

It makes no sense—I was so small—
but I know I was alone
when I found the bees: they crawled,
golden, velvet as bees are,
through a glass tube inserted
in the wall.
I knew their tread—
intending footsteps on my arm
and on my neck;
they drew a line so sweet I curled inside,
all leaf.

I was caramel-headed, patent-shoed;
a velvet collar striped my camel coat.
The costume gave me entrée to
the glass hive honeycomb, the wax near-fluid and alive,
and at its heart, the Queen, a giantess in dense gold Matter.

Were those her eggs?
Was that larva?

The furry bees queued inside the tube;
beyond the hive, the floor was paced with taxidermied paws,
and clatter rose to break the diorama case
that kept them from attack upon
the human drones that brought them death.

I felt as if I'd stumbled on some truth,
and silent shrieking birds and tawny-coated
cougars under glass,
would one day join the exodus of bees.
I held my breath lest someone thoughtless thought to intervene
and shut their egress.

## Airing Cupboard

At the back of the top shelf,
on clean slats of pine,
against the insulated water heater and
warming blankets, I unwrap a towel.
Inside are a red rubber bag and a white hose
with plastic nozzle. I lay them aside
and open a grey hardback marriage manual,
leaf through the red-with-blue-veins colour-plate genitals,
search further a-field and find the marriage bed itself,
the sheets pulled tight, a nightdress laid out
across lace pillows: curtains closed, window open to the damp.

When it's over, she changes the sheets, stores away
the bed for another month—but wait—
here are his letters on thin blue paper:
*My darling, I need you!* And discover deeper,
cached in the niche behind the water tank
with head bent and knees clasped,
where wooden walls retain the scent of forest,
the marriage itself:
because they cannot agree what's to be done with it,
and unlike an abandoned child,
it will not die.

## Connection

I was never a dealer—
I wore an Indian sweater
and green hair ribbons, and ate tinned jam
with a spoon.
When I looked out the window,
I found orchards of greengage plums:
caterpillars tented their leaves
in gauzy detail, and then reinvented.

I was never a dealer—
but my brother and I knelt in the grass
of the flats and picked magic mushrooms.
I kept mine in a tin
while men from black limousines
tucked up their sleeves
and grazed the fields clean.

I was never a dealer—
but when the counterweight slipped on the drill rig,
I sat in a car with my boyfriend
and stared at some pills.
It's okay, he said—and I hated him—
I know exactly how it must feel
when somebody dies
and you loved them.

# Tug

At the end of the afternoon, when the sun released
our burned shoulders, and the last log rider
beached and sat on a blanket with the fried chicken
and potato salad and gherkins,
the uncles stood, fists crushing cake.
Muscular as walrus, they were heavy as anvils,
smoothly unwound as seals.

From the trunk of one of the Chevys, the cousins brought out
rope, and we ran to take sides—me with my dad for anchor:
he was more than a match for the bulk of his brothers.
My mother joined in, cardigan sleeves rolled,
hair in a scarf,
while the aunts—majestic in dresses, ripe-bosomed—
travailed and trammelled with dishes.

When it was time, we hauled, my father and I and my mother
  and brother
and the numberless cousins:
the uncles tugged landward, but the tide lapped at our legs,
and the moon, the planets, the stars doubled in water
and pulled hard, too,
through the uncoiling sea,
the dead along with us,
in their too tight good clothes.

## Red Sweater

I was the one with the red zippered sweater
and red shoes and overalls
and a heart red as fire.
God above couldn't have me
though the unnumbered worlds
ran through my brain in numeric swirls.

God knows, I loved the garden,
the worms in the cabbages,
the plum at the fence, but I did not like
the boy next door who said,
*You have to see.* I grew bored,
looked at his bum
and thought of the depot downtown
where a machine dispensed aluminum slugs
punched with my name.

That warm afternoon in the shed,
while the bulldozer operator's son
pulled at his plumage,
and the fields wailed with cows,
my red shoes ran to the fence: I edged
underneath and he shouted,
*You're scared!*
and I called back,
*No* man *hath seen God...*

At the outdoor cinema, I crouched in the grass
and my boyfriend gave me a tab:
then we took off our clothes
and discovered our rest
with the golden Tibetan gods.

## Sixteen

I'd long had tendrils of
a ferny feeling,
and I'd read the books:
a boy would push his tongue inside my mouth,
and bring me close to wisdom and to death.

With entry would come love, a perfect fit:
a gift much like my mother's velvet dress,
in elegance and touch—piano music:
I'd only have to practice, then to use it.

But when a boy approached me on the porch,
my father flicked the night light on and off—
a signal from a shore retreating fast.
My pink and white
angora sweater slipped—
first shoulders, then a breast:

I'd never thought a task
so gently could unmask
and open with a kiss—

slow barges on a river's
restless movement.

# Virgin

It was summer.
I sat in the Sprott Shaw typing class,
the feeling all day like
metal and brick,
a hook on a pole
to open the top pane
of a tall window.

Blood clots fell like apples
from a torn pocket of a torn apron.
I ran to the washroom.

My mother brought towels from home;
they typed on and on, in the next room.

In the hospital ward,
the nurses, nuns, brought me a pan.
They pushed the bed
along a corridor
and into a room.

I won't hurt you, the doctor said.
Tighten up, he said. Your breasts,
they're big for your size. Ha ha.

I wore a green plaid nightie and jacket
to greet him,
but I walked away through the halls
without them.

# Bear

Like me you wear a heavy coat
of flesh; like me you are hungry:
you travel the woods
and tread through sunlight to smell the sea.

How alike we are, and yet you flee
my embrace, my bite into
the muscles of your neck.

What if my paw as it cups your head,
is the hand that helps,
and the snout that snuffles your armpit
only wants your scent?

It could be worse—
you could be ignored.

Each night when I turn
in my bed of leaves and look up,
I hear your voice: sometimes it sings
(sometimes it weeps).

So why should you resist
the sincerity of this

kiss?

# Elephant

It is enough
to hold your hand when we step from the curb,
to feel the smiles of the other walkers rain down.
Some shrink in fear
when the shadow of an airplane's wing darkens the stream,
but the rest is as we desire, although
an old woman near me falls behind.

But we are moving towards the brass band:
my father plays tuba,
my brother the trumpet,
I have a toy ukulele on a string
and my name printed on a card upside down.

Your grip crushes mine, but
ahead is the band shell,
and warm loaves of bread,
and comb honey, and the pains in my hands
are only because of time.

I can feel what I like because
my mind fastens with beauty—
as if I were a girl who knew where she's going
and to what end in this unreeling company,
your spirit around me like a spangled cloak,
for the day when we reach the elephant and I will ride.

## Wardrobe

I come to the door, the building
large and old; the walls groan,
the elevator displays a taillight.
Upstairs, I lie on the bed—so many flights of snow.
My childhood knocks at the window,
relentless and pure in intent
as the stranger who called
when my mother died, and said
*Hello, hello, who's calling me?*
night after night.

On top of the wardrobe
there's a long grey snout
that pushes a box to the edge.

Rat—you think you can frighten me
with your shoves,
but there are people in all the houses
on all the streets
who will never give up their love.

# Hotel

That was the year of hotel rooms,
bad judgment, some salesman with a model contract
in Prince George,
and I was all about irony: a mini-skirt,
hair like a veil, but my home was the library.

My home was the library, not a cheap bedspread and
some guy with a moustache saying, *My wife can't understand me.*
I had only been curious;
in the dark, the yellow bedside lamp
was damp and furious: my mini-skirt fell off,
and the Vietnam vet in the next room, cried: *Don't worry,*
*we don't carve up chicks*
*personally.*

God said—it was God's voice on the radio—in the guise of
my school friend, Tom—a DJ—
God or Tom—said on the radio: *Please call.*
So I leapt up, all reasonable and not confrontational,
not at all stoned, and I phoned.
Dear Tom, wherever you are
I'm telling you now—
I ran down the hall to a parking lot sign
that read *Full.*

The policeman who pulled me over
said I was going too slow. Oh.

There was also the year of the knife, the year of the gun,
the year God's voice whispered, again and again,
*What are you trying to do,*
*kill yourself?* But this was the year of hotel rooms,
when I looked into corners nobody swept and felt
their pull; when I wore my hair like a pall,
and didn't know how lovely I was at all.

## Fidelity

It was dark, yet the gorse was yellow
and green above the little stream
we sieved for drinking water.
Indoors, on the bed, I took
your knife, scored my palm and passed
the blade to you.
The ancient stones nearby, crabbed in broken circles,
the mothy bull, the red deer just about to butt
and send a rutting roar across the glen,
agreed that blood's been shed before
to prove a point.

You scarred your hand and when
I pressed the welling lines to mine, you calmed,
lay down your broken-heartedness in sleep.
Inside a poem's no place to fix
a spiral loosed between us then
and since; but I would always
mix your blood with mine.

Though you're intent on courting distance,
I have a means to find you
through the red-deer witness,
the stones that never stop their starry
turn; the bull's seed-lives, spilled in a womb
and on the grassy turf which cleft hooves drive—
these can be touched;

just like the heart that breathes in life and rest,
or apples store their seeds
to feed the wayfarer
now, alone, or with a company who finds her
worthy.

## Deer

So many years and they always return
to stand in the rain where I can watch them
from the baby's room;
everything's green
and the cats step out
and listen for the owl's swoop over the trees.

The deer browse the leaves;
when a car passes by a mile away,
they lift their heads
and then resume.

Something in this that is the same
as when I woke late at night
in my grandparents' house,
apple trees and plum trees outside,
the wind crowing to find us,
the shiver of doors part-opening,
the whisper of parents downstairs—

and all the children in all their rooms
staring at ceilings,
to watch shadows find
small animals
they will someday have to bury
in the morning.

## 14 Washington Place

No one told me the wind that blew
the windows open, was an apron unpinned,
unhooked garters,
stockings unfurled,
when grief bloomed full
as skirts in my New York rooms.

I got up, looked out, watched men rummage
the skips and break glass;
trucks scraped metal sparks;
the drunks, sandwiched
between stiff sheets of cardboard,
slept hard, their bodies chutes
of loose cans and vomit.

The windows in the building opposite,
fluttered light: someone's feet toed a sill,
and behind her a kettle silvered.
Nobody said, but the radio
tuned all night could not block the smoky sighs
when the Shirtwaist factory girls joined hands
and jumped.
Overhead, the night birds sprawled an open sky,
but the air above the street grew
dense with plunging bodies.

Yet when I searched beyond the parapet,
I found trees, pure water,
a stroll of riverbank,
and Solomon's carpet descending from above
as if in consideration of
an indiscriminate, timely act of love.

# SOUL

I have to be still and the water
has to be quiet; it can't rain,
and there can be no sunlight or darkness
to fill the well, no moonlight to distract
with the thought I might hear a footstep
and see a face in the water over my shoulder.

The shadow of a fish makes a green sword,
and when the fish slips elsewhere,
there's broken crockery
and a child with struts of bones,
cabled and draperied.

And beside it's the mirror-twin of the dog
I found at the end of the pier in Brigus South,
tied by a rope to a stone,
the dog black and green in the water,
the stone already
incised with weed.

The dog's mouth opened, its opaque
eyes cleared and it cried: *I didn't deserve this.*
*See where the village plants its headstones.*
*How strange that graves overlook the harbour entrance;*
*and the scenic shacks, and the headland of foaming grass—*
*don't trust any of it.*

My daughter and her friend in their winter boots
smashed the shore ice. I said a prayer for the dog,
and we left.

And so there is one thing only I need to know
when I lean over the well to enquire, and it is
Who will put the light of kindness into our children's
faces, and how will they know?

*For P.K.*

## If I knew the horses better
I could speak to them calmingly:
they gaze at me with such eyes,
they have familiar faces,
as if they are the dead who come to meet me
each night.
Not that I mind—the dead
know me better than anyone alive—
I remember their youths,
and they mine.

Perhaps my own nature is hidden from me?
I, too, may have hooves, and the hair that swings in my eyes
could be a mane: how would I know?

Those beautiful grasses: the scents with which they cushion
me at night—like an excellent mattress,
like a countryside of hope
where everyone lives in warm houses
and eats an egg at breakfast—
*but when were there such times?*

What a message the dead bring, at night, when they
are grazing; when they tiptoe through the minds
of their loved ones, who can't help but call to them,
because the soft nuzzle of the nose
of a dear one, cannot be replaced.

Oh grief, oh the pleasure of living in a world
built solely for the happiness
of finding everything
that will pass.

I am afraid to startle the horses:
they are stabled, quiet at last
after such a long night of calling them.
One by one they entered at dawn from over the hill,
from a grove of trees, from the shelter of rocks—
had they just given birth to their foals?
I do not know the ways and means and reasons of horses,
but they are safe with me, out of the snow.
I feed them; brush the painful burrs and spears from their coats.

Come, dear horses, the nights are long,
and there are few like me
who truly love you.
Such horrors are inflicted on horses, my dear ones:
you have seen your companions bludgeoned,
you have witnessed them eaten
by those who do not understand
that horses are their only hope of salvation.
The proof is in the clearing skies,
a pool of reflection on our lifted faces.

The stream we search for is cold:
I am here alone,
and I remain as always—
no tufted ears, no hardness melted from my eyes,
though I'd prefer to be more like you
and at peace.

# Hours

The horses are stopped at a wall;
the driver steps down.

The horses eat grass between stones;
their hooves remain sharp.

They do not count the hours;
they breathe air broken by whirring scythes.

The footfalls of branches climb to a window;
the horses' hooves cut steps.

My life waits, upside down, with folded wings;
my thoughts are bushes that rustle with frightened quails.

Anything is possible,
except to disbelieve.

## Considering Apples

I must put on my shoes,
pick up the bag by my side;
I must remember who I have to meet
and when; time is passing:
there are trains and long prepared assignations,
a pantechnicon of kitchens, beds, lovers—God knows what—
but most of all there is a company of friends.

They are travelling across the sky,
they are travelling with coats slung
over their shoulders,
with extra shoes in soft bags with clever straps—
everything arranged so they do not feel the weight.
They journey with dogs and cats as emissaries—
these scout ahead; they converse with animals in foreign countries—
preparation for the visit of these dignitaries.

Everywhere they are expected and right on time.

I'm so late—I must catch up—night after night, trying to sleep,
and day after day, endeavouring to wake;
and most of all to keep my temper over
the waste of all the beautiful apples
in abandoned trees—
you'd think someone would stop to pick them.

But even fallen on the ground,
and to be close to their souls,
they must be feeding someone
in return for their time
on earth.

*For Martha*

**Only yesterday I was reading**
the Greek poets—those transitional asphodels,
the tinkling unattainable light—
and learned that *Art and poetry help us
to die.* But of course Engonopoulos spoke
of our crippled times.
And all the while you were
escaping the warm hands
of your family, you were thinking
*Is it springtime?*
and you were back on the road to Parikia,
and I was about to meet you for the first time.

I'd forgotten the blue veins of your forehead,
the tremble of your hands when you borrowed
cigarettes; the way a star glittered
above the open stone corridors we wandered
to a hill among the trees and cats—and we begged
time from the stars, moon and sea.
But in the rain on the ferry,
the island dropped veils in the waters,
and in the hotel the police came:
who is there to know that story now?

Some will think that a friend is not eternally present—
*but it may be and it may be*
that we will meet again on a thyme-scented road,
the cats Chaos and Phaedra with us,
the cold wind off the Aegean unravelling like smoke
around your silver earrings and black hair.

Your footsteps ring wet,
grow quiet among cypress,
and for me, there's a smudge of dusk here:
but this is the place,
in a drift of dry brush
undone by the hidden red garment
of butterflies,

that you unwrap from your rest
and blaze.

## Chamonix

I could see when we rode the cable car
up the Aiguille de Midi, the white razor line
Anselme and Eduard had skied:
I was thinking of Anselme—
how he *had* to say Eduard's name.

It made us weep
when he spoke to us of Eduard.

I thought of the summoning forces
of mountains,
and of crevassed glaciers,
dark with trespass,
and that night dreamed that a young man entered
our train as it reached the Mont Blanc massif—

and the blue rock of his face,
and his hair black with ice,
and he shone—how to say what he was?

How do you not let go of the essence?
I asked him, meaning
the upthrust of earth,
the stars on their travels,
himself and all marvels.

*I keep this in mind*
*and I trace it again and again,*
he told me—
and sketched a golden figure of eight
on its side
in the air.

Infinity.

I love the little birds
that fill the topped fir;
their beaks snip pine cones,
unstitch a shower of burnished pods
lightly falling.

I love the yellow-bellied birds,
small as pull knobs,
that blow all at once from the apple tree
like yellow transparents.

I love the returners, year after year
to the knothole in the cedar siding,
rapping, endeavouring to penetrate
to dark tar paper and beyond;

and the flicker tapping love notes
on the metal chimney;
and the nuthatch who leaps from a bush
that scrapes my window;

and the woods themselves,
waving, full of questions
amidst the chittering *I do,*
*I do, I do.*

I love these small marriages.
I love the restless hearts
that survive.

That hummingbird winks green;
the sky's blue eye blinks awareness: *okay;*
the heron's paper legs
cut a fine pencil drawing:
how many wing strokes
to complete the picture?

*Who who* else?—the owl.
Below its questions there's a crash of deer;
coiled thimbleberry and wind-shredded groundcover
spring—how else could it be?

*How else* but in a high meadow
from where the sea is a thumb of silver,
and the grasses bleed sapphire and yellow,
and the pink bees bumble through moss.

Can a songbird believe in its tune,
sing and not know a word?
So beautiful: this cry for someone it will
never know.

## Wild Roses

Your face writes
and I can read—

how could it be said more clearly?

Wild roses grow
in wild soil,

and they *will* bloom
more brief than beautiful.

## Satin Flower

Now that grief no longer
climbs the night stairs,

I can say that the heart
goes on its distant loping anyway,

and the mind continues
to paint scenery.

Some of those pictures are dark,
some hesitant—

like the way the pink, timid soul
is said to hover above the body
and interpret.

And so—
it's springtime on a mountain:

I walk with friends
between pale bars of alder,

and there's a flower that spreads
purple satin sheeting,

its leaves like spikes of grass,
its petals open just for a day—
open to whatever comes,

and open to whatever comes.

## Fawn Lilies

Just before we looked back at
the reservoir and the sluice gate with its lock,
the sun angled on the glimmer of water
like a key.

There were lilies
at the foot of trees and where rock
fell away at the edge
of the footpath.

I remember current in bloom,
and red leaves of Oregon grape,
and pink buds on a grey bush,
plushy in all that gloom—
but the lilies
are fifty years gone.

Ghosts and lilies
rise from the ferns,
flow down the green bluff
(how they manage their increase
I cannot say),
but the lilies turn mottled and sallow.

No reason, now, to recall
the strangeness of facing dawn,
their new white clothes
spilled in the hollow.

## Summer

You open the sleeping bag,
the zipper cool against your legs—
so many nights with nothing
but the moon that roves like a shining stone.
What's the point of running away?
The bodies of ancestors roam freely;
and you can hear the scrape of suitcases down the street,
the straps unclip.

But you lean from the window,
let down the knotted sheets
(no one awake in the house but you)
to pad down a dock in bare feet
and stand in your nightdress,
water mouthing quiet hulls,
oars lapsed in oarlocks,

and throw a handful of pebbles
to stir the sea—
bioluminescence like a fall
of petals all night;
so that when you return,
blossoms have blown in,

your tiredness emptied
like an apple tree
unhitching its leaves
from the convoy of bones

to learn how to branch
and to bend without ending.

And now I can't come with you—
now they take their tools
and dismantle the scaffolding;
now they are masked and gowned.

The light shudders where they move—
they do not hear your innocence.
Now the ship has turned back;
there are windows on shore,
sun on glass.

And there, between columns,
angels stream to the portholes.
Their high notes tear you from safety
and fashion cloth made from your skin.
Shall I put it on? Or remember
that inside the most beautiful creatures of the sea,
the brain is a pulse without memory.

## When I close my eyes

horses pass by the foot of the drive,
the dog creeps into the house,
a fly spins on its back on the carpet;

and in my private dark I remember the moon,
and your shoulders are under my hands.

A rowboat leaves the dock,
sunlight laps the back of my neck,
an island lifts anchor and moves closer.

I should sit there now
and sing as I meant to,
to the end of the lake
and into the marsh
where the waterbirds dive.

When I close my eyes,
the palms of my hands
become heavy;
they shut around stones:
and when they release,
they show me what I have lost
and what I can never recover.

*For Susan*

## She sits in a field listening to shrikes,

waiting for antelope to step through wet grasses,
hoping she'll find a buffalo, a small one, quietly grazing.
This buffalo does not want to be discovered:
it carries in its gristle clots of light, deep lightning slashes,
and it's perfectly made to run.
It cannot imagine a museum any more than the girl who fin-
gers a grass stalk and folds it to fit in a pocket,
can dream she won't be here long.
She doesn't see the sky is full of horses
and all she has to do to be happy
is find the one that will never surrender its speed.


❧


To begin—
ask the wolves to stop their nose through drawers,
ask that the dogs curl up at the end of the bed,
ask that the birds find something to eat,
ask that the young find each other,

that they be entranced by each others' faces,
ask that they find the doors;

ask that they take up swimming,
ask that they hear music,
ask for an antelope,
ask for the end of war.


❧


All the children out of their apartments,
their mothers in black coats, their fathers in black shoes,
the older boys with mattresses,
the older girls with deck chairs:

I shouldn't have to tug your sleeve,
I shouldn't have to tug at your hem,
I shouldn't have to ease you along with my snout,
I shouldn't have to tell you the story—
you should know by now who I am
and come quietly.

It is not the fault of the trees
or the birds building nests—
they carry and construct,
they weave and thatch.

No one is looking,
no stars are vigilant.

I wouldn't advise waiting,
I wouldn't advise wasting your time,
I wouldn't advise gathering apples
to carry in an apron,
I wouldn't advise running,
I wouldn't advise stumbling,
I wouldn't advise calling for help,
I wouldn't advise it
if it can't help in the end—

and that mountain, snow and blossom—
all were placed just to bring you joy.


❧


The horse in the lane
wants to have its say:
how patient it is;
decades pass while it halts
between shafts.

The horse breathes into
a nosebag and waits for
hands to find the pearl
in its grey coat. I've got it now—

you are no ordinary horse:
I must nerve myself
to examine what you have in your wagon:

milk, I thought once, but the clanging
might not be metal pails but
human chains
on the way to the smelter.

༺

She carries it like a chick in her hands;
her rings form the periphery she'll allow it.
Sometimes it's her daughter's voice, sometimes her husband's.
She keeps it outdoors where the wind blows it clean
and rain settles the dust.
She shows the top of its head to her friends.
It never lifts out; it never takes her life.
She'll not give it up.
It's hers as much as the horses she rode
in a tale told by a teller who wanders off in the middle,
the fire still glowing, the children waiting to learn the end.
*Hu Hu*

**In a dark wood,**
trees surround you, but
their branches fill with birds—
a wing; an iridescent eye—
such fire as the phoenix brings.
The woods grizzle with rain;
light drains, and is cold.
You are song, although you've lost
your singing.
Be your ears, until your voice takes hold
and you can view
blue wings, a flash of gold.
Everything is made:
put your tongue out to the rain
and claim.

# THE STORYTELLERS ON THEIR CARPETS

## Soul Mouth

The bed kneels in front of me,
the window swings open
and pushes the curtains—
they are pink, with tiny roses:
lengths of extra material
fold in the sewing drawer.

I hold my breath:
my eyes grow warm inside.

A pair of bloodless hands
in the corner, angles
for my throat—
my grandmother's stitches
on the pillowcase
spell them away.

What can they want
with my small soul?

Soul mouth: you breathe in
and loveliness goes;
you breathe out and blossoms
arc the walls.

You breathe in—
all ears shut to all cries;
you breathe out and children sit
at coloured tables
unwrapping their lunches.

You breathe in, and letters and numbers
fly to the back of your throat;
you breathe out and the storytellers
hum on their carpets.

I rest in the pause between—
never awake, never asleep.

## Wasps' Nest

They hang it in the crook of a tree,
a soul tree, and fill it with paper
and ash like a piñata.
Then the wasps arrive
and chew the bark into spit,
and they spin out in flights,
stingers alert.

Do not think of meat;
do not sweat in the heat.
They crawl over your stillness,
they burrow in the creases of your clothes,
they make love to you until your soul
is in fragments and it hurts.

Your body swells, your shoes
fly off; then you fly too—
a soul shard all on its own—
until you come to your senses,

the earth far below,

and you drop
back into your home—
the fork of the tree
where your grandfather
has lit the paper cells
of the wasps' nest
to glory,
and set them free.

## Christmas Eve

I waited all night
while snow piled on the window sills,
the heating vents drew breath,
a stray cat finished its milk;
a tree stood dark
in the living room
and each house I'd ever live in
listened at the doors.

We waited for the stranger
late off the train,
who'd set off on his journey
with a duffle bag,
his boots laced up,
North Atlantic salt
webbed in his frozen hair,
and with Jack Frost fingernails
scoring the railcar glass.

*Baby Jesus: I hope you're awake, too.*
*I've a pillow, a comforter,*
*and so many questions.*
*I wrap my soul*
*in a blanket and*
*lie in the dark listening*
*for hoof-beats on the roof*
*and for your reply.*

In the hallway,
the linoleum squeaked,
my heart enclosed the bedroom
and then the entire night sky.
I prayed to each star embedded there
for gold, frankincense and myrrh enough
that all the children of the world
would never be lost or cold again,
never again on Christmas Eve,
and I would get to open the door
for Uncle Mel.

## Soul Dressing

The sleeves are short and tight,
and you dislike the pig nostrils
and the bland cow-frown
of its brows.
Did you make a mistake
when you chose this soul
from the closet?

But the one with gold sewn
into the lining must swim
for its life, and it might go down,
it might, glittering, drown.

When god's fire pours forth
like gasoline, you'll have to ignore
the soul's hurt, and tear off the garment
whatever the cost
to the heart you were born with—

like a boy with two sticks
that could be real swords
or the crutches he needs
to make it home
through deepening snows,

but who breaks them over his knees instead
to kindle a fire
because he is cold unto death
now.

# Firebox

I pull on my shoes,
do up the straps:

in the bathroom next door,
the slither of razor strop.

Find brown paper to draw on,
tug a blanket
under the table, add
the pear tree,
the plum tree,
the sugar apple wintering,
the crabapple,
the roses, the roses.

Green woods grow,
the window frame rattles:

all around me now, the huff
of foot-padding dogs,

and fingers on the window glass writing
*Mene mene tekel upharsin.*

From the basement—
the cough smell of apples;
in the front room—
a smoke of prayers:
the roof unpeels to
the heavens,
the furnace door opens,
the firebox roars.

God, in your certainty,
have you built all this just for me?

## Prayer Room

In the night, when the sky holes open
and flights of crows dismember the planets—
when everyone is gone—
I know what death is:
it travels from the heart of matter
like a tattoo needle,
ferocious.

When I am tethered in a pew,
men who stir change in their pockets
wearing black summoning shoes,
lead me to the prayer room
on a dog leash of fear.
I kneel, elbows on seat,
face at the barred chair-back
in a bondage of grief
like wet sheeting,
like the laving of teeth.

And I cannot find my way
to God's kingdom
when there are no doors
and no windows,
although my dear ones
count on it—
they want my soul to be saved.

My father and uncles
build good boats
and good houses—
safe refuge—
with strong planks and straight nails.
But I will have to wade
through a thousand
devious spirits lapping
the kneelers, the weepers
before I know it
for my own.

## Winter Fever

The first snowball
becomes the moon
or a dream
or the lamp beside the bed,
or a blind white dog
scraping frost from the window.
I'm glad to be wanted,
here and not here.

When I'm awake
in the silence,
the blind dog's fur
blows like corn
in a field.
I walk into the field,
away from the ache in my bones,
because somebody's knocking
for me to come outside
in the snow,
and they won't wait.

## Passover

The bed like a clothespin bag,
the children—head to tail.
The one in the middle
sees the curtains spill
a thief's shadow onto the blankets.

The biggest kick and turn;
they fight from under the thief's duffle.
The smallest goes to the window—
nothing in the street

but Jesus perched on top
of a telephone pole.

Back in bed, the one with a cough
rumples sheets,
tosses aside pillows.

Death's in the neighbourhood
spiriting bodies out the door

in its slippers.

# All Winter He Constructs

The keel takes shape in the house,
the bone of it overhead,
the swimming dark below,
a body already separated—

sea-silt in its mouth,
a tongue tarry with salt,
hands scraping the boards.

The splash of the paddle
smacks the door—
twice for the dark kitchen,
three times for the water jug.
The walls bend with steam,
thick ice at the windows,
trestles cradling the keel.

With each sweep of the plane,
the soul curls its shavings
into a wave's kettle,
the keel like a fish knife
to filet water.

Like a song in the chest
too big to contain indoors
when the wall comes down
for the summer.

# The Ferry

I get on board: portholes yawn,
the car deck swallows,
families tumble from cars,
the children's feet clang on metal stairs,
the doors of telephone boxes accordion—
people stopping in to call goodbye.

Everyone runs from deck to deck,
compartments close and seal,
log-thick ropes sink to the deep
and the ferry soughs from the slip,
the ship's sides cool.

This time I hold my mother's hand,
I lean against my father.
When sailors swarm to the lifeboats,
my brother offers chewing gum
and a comic book.
I turn the pages to the end,
discover what happens and when—

my arms hooked over a life belt,
the sea before me,
my face alight with the ferry spark of the soul.

## Natural Disasters

It rains all night
until the bed floats
and you stand on it
waving at the others
in small lifeboats—

the tigers and lions,
the anteaters snuffling the thwarts,
at the piled up
and wingless,

at the dogs nosing the sails,
at the untethered horses
stomping the planks—

at the saved world
fleeing.

No fire or brimstone—
just the rain in your sleeves,
the shameless wet bottom
of your pajamas,
no toothbrush,
no mother, no father.

It's a beautiful planet—
its green and blue soul
like the secret pinion feathers
of a phoenix.

You wave
at its gold, at its coal seams,
at the glisten of salmon,
at its creekbed gravel—
its digging and shifts
like the flight of the heron
on night watch, on dawn watch.

And you breathe
through the night,
waving onwards
the owls at the prows,
the elephants and bison,

at the reluctance to drown
which has seized all creation
and forced you to listen
to its cries.

## Space Talk

This is no ship—
not even a lifeboat—
the planet is a plate
set spinning through the cosmos.
How I got on board this not-ship
is anyone's guess.
Someone needed a carpenter
or a shipwright or a soulful partner
to cling to the stem and look out...

Anyway: I'm here and it's time
we spoke. Plate-mates, we're together;
why not come close?
We've no landmarks—
we're at sea, like Columbus
Magellan, Vasco de Gama
who scoured maps
by lamplight.

In old age
everyone dies
except us:
we're too busy spinning and looking at stars
and following comet trails;
we're too irresponsible to lose heart
and die.

I can't buy shoes
or a large suitcase.
My credit cards spill
onto wet ground.
Meantime,
my companions are hobbled nearby
eating grass—
their stomachs churn out replicas
of coins in the sunshine—
you think you've got troubles!
When I was a child,
I ate sand to be different.
Even before I was born
I swallowed a chain of gold.
It's all nonsense,
but in the night when the owls
fall silent,
I want to go wherever
I'm understood—
with all the friends
who troop through my bedroom.
It's a regular stop—
don't misunderstand—
you don't need to wake
or quit snoring,
just look me in the eyes

while you dream,
and come.

❦

I have parcels tied over my shoulders,
and in my hands—packets of sandwiches,
flasks of tea.
I could go anywhere:
my blanket is folded neatly.
I want to tell you how it began,
my story,
but I'm reluctant to burn your ears
with my scandals.
Without belief,
it's a hard road:
I could show you my feet—
everything I've learned
is in their soles—
but I have to run.

❦

Is it poetry to talk
when nobody listens?
Everyone knows what they feel,
so what's the point?
Anyone can pull up a soapbox

and pass the time.
A poem is the weather;
its cold touches the bones,
its heat the genitals—
don't deny it—
you look to verses and worse
when you're stung.
Step onto this iceberg:
when we reach a melting centre,
that oasis of zygote
just like we planned,
there's a birth—
no matter that I'm old.
Not everything is about sex—
even this good cigar
for my birthday.
Sometimes I just want to smoke
and remember Vesuvius
before I stand too still,
freeze to death.

This plate-form is moving
and we're all on it:
ice-craft or raft or mechanical genius—
it's all good company.

❧

No need to lock up
or learn combinations.
I've forgotten my passwords,
but I can pass anywhere
with empty saddlebags—
you know what I'm saying?
You—troubadour under the apple tree—
you're a bum
but you sound lovely.
Your eyes are pure rain,
and those dappled leaves
above you pattern
your ragged clothing.
I wonder what you really
are up to—burying treasure
in the roots of pippins,
peeling bananas to show you've
travelled.
No one else knows these roads;
but your price is heavy.
*Listen to my songs,* you say:
*Listen and you will fall in love.*
Ho ho. Not when I'm on my way
to the bank
to fill my stomach with paper.
What did I say?
I'm too irresponsible to lose heart,

too busy spinning, and gazing at stars.
Come closer, everyone:
just look me in the eyes
and I'll go anywhere.

# The Pupils of Plato

She was a pupil of Plato's: she felt nothing for the table in front of her. Somewhere beyond the veils of atmosphere, extraterrestrial planetary life spun on. Nothing to do with her, but it was a comfort to consider the perfection of table. No gum stuck under the edge; no child, with a dog at its knees, across from her with a book. She could give herself a new name, if she liked.

He was a pupil of Plato's: verbs past, present, and future fluted through his brain. The world of forms meant nothing remained still. He told his secret to no one. But his prayer ascended like smoke. There were cigarettes, cut in half, which he gave to the other prisoners. The prisoners were in chains, but they could strike fire from the materials they'd been given, if they were willing to go without food. He was followed by a dog as he walked up and down through the cave crying, I love my teacher, I love him above all others.

The pupils of Plato made a school. Its shabby door and windows were blocked with bricks, but you could see the worn threshold where Plato and the pupils had passed back and forth. When Plato taught outdoors, the pupils waved small fans and nets never harming the insects they captured, simply examining the *potential* of the insects to sting. Harm and release.

## Why are you here, my dear students?

You should be filling your minds with literature,
your souls with the love of the world.
Why aren't you on my doorstep, so full of longing
for poetry that you'll suffer in the cold
until I let you in and reveal my secrets?

Have I told you my story?
All night I wrote in a kitchen overrun
with mice to have a poem worthy of my teacher.
The small black mice had a heyday with the garbage;
they broke the rubber seal of the refrigerator
and skated along the shelves: what mouldered cheeses they found,
what aged vegetables!

What a trial it was to remain with my back to them
and hear their scrabble, the testing twitter of a hundred
mouse beats, and write my semblance of poetry. What else
did I have to bring to my master?
What have *you* given me, I ask you,
but your faith that I can solve the world's enmity
to poets; that within the grading system there's a key
I keep just out of reach.

The golden door, my dear ones, is near:
don't listen to a word I say; sleep on the doorstep
of a poet—there's a certain coming and going,
the passage of all the other poets who visit.

You must suffer the depredations of vermin
until you can hear them.
Oh, *they'll say*, here's a new one, what will we do
with him or her—lift them up
and bring them in for soup?

When you revive and your lungs are sufficiently warmed
and full of literature, and when the fragments of your hearts
reveal themselves as letters
kept safely just for you, then hold a pen and begin your addresses.

Oh, my dear ones, my beloved
students who I fail constantly to inspire in the classroom,
only then
will you know what it is I have to teach you.

**Dear my students, once more I must talk to you:**
it is important, please listen.
You are caught in the gaze of a bull.
You must know this in order to protect yourselves.
Do not run; do not look back; think only of the flowers in your hands,
the innocence with which you entered these pastures.
Remember the heat of the day, the sun on your shoulders
and the blessing that sprang to your lips when you paused
to consider the flow of hills.

The white flowers you've gathered inside the fence
may drop from your hands, and the garland may loosen—
but the bull will not reach you in time.
Your disappearance will be only one of many
incomprehensibilities to the dull bull mind.

Don't reconsider, don't have doubts
since something in you may desire
the bull's attention:
there is such credence and force in its dimness
and how may I put this—where else would you find such large balls?
This dark and pendulous sack could be the engendering
fount of the world—
it is not: the bull's semen produces only imagos of itself.

Your intrusion, the flickering quality of your souls' casing,
is like the bee that stumbles into the bull's ringed nose.
You remind it of its chains, unhooked now, but waiting.
Someone will come, unlatch the gate,

shoo the timid cows away and with block and tackle
reattach those shackles,
milk the bull of its seed direct.
It will be helpless, furiously unscrewed,
disarmed by the gush of its power
and to no real end (dear students, forgive the pun).

This is not your business: your task is to reach the other side
of the pasture alive.
You are too valuable to waste, my dear ones.
You must walk away now quietly,
and try to remember your poems.

**When I used to walk here, on visits to my friend,**
she would say: Someone who lives nearby is your twin;
many times I've rushed up to find it isn't you,
hair the colour of Fall leaves,
coat toggled and looped against the wind.
It's not an easy wind; it tingles the nostrils,
it knifes the sealed and ironed edge of comfort.
From a distance
it conveys the gaze of wild animals—
shall we go to them, our feet in snow,
our eyes crinkled against the light?

That's my friend; an unusual woman.
There's some depth here I've not explained,
occasioned by a whiff of pinewoods
from her Hungarian name
and in her desire to climb
the cliffs and steeps of mountains in thin shoes.

Her brother plays the violin,
he's in love with my cousin.
All this love frisking down windy streets,
twirling the headachy leaves of plane trees.

Today a woman finds me in the street
where my friend once lived and says:
I know the house in which you will
complete your life. It isn't far,
you can afford it.

Never have I felt such joy
as when I escape—leap the back steps running.

The woman ahead of me is slower;
her hair's tangled on her shoulders,
her duffle coat's fastened
against the falling temperature.
Look, I say, to the face that turns to mine—
I've caught up to you at last,
it must be time.

**We are deep in the labyrinth now, Ariadne,**
and I'm thinking there are conversations we should have had
before I began this journey.
Are you still here? If I tug, will you hold to your end of the string,
or have you embarked on some other dalliance
while I'm lost in the dark except for this link
to your heart?

I didn't ask who made the Minotaur in the dark
of your father's kingdom: people blame the gods,
but I'm the one who has to scramble
over the bones of the young.
I knew many of them—friends, cousins—
knew them better than
I know you.
Ariadne, have there been other men?
Women don't often tell the truth about their friends;
but if the sword breaks at first blow
I'll know what you've done.

What have I done?
I should have killed your father,
would have if you hadn't begged me
to 'consider your feelings.'
*Theseus*, you said, *it's not just about us.*
So thoughtful: are your hands painted
with the blood of my friends?

You must like this blood sport:
no girl can be as innocent as you purport.
I make discoveries in the labyrinth
I'd not make in Athenian light—
once I've run the monster to ground,
I'll put everything right.
Ready, or not, Ariadne, *fee-fi-fo-fum*
here I come.

**When Scheherazade went to the sultan, did she say:**
What is your question? No, dear friends,
she gave him the answer to the question
he didn't know he had.

All my life in this cube of height and depth,
I have pushed my mind against a wall.
There have been answers—
the sine curve and its description of a circle,
and the sound with which the world was formed.
And all the while I've been walking, holding hands with you,
I've never asked what called to you in the mists,
and what the voice said
that brought the sound of oars roaring in the fog.
There was singing inside of you
while I was in my cube
testing the walls thinking
we will meet again…

As Scheherazade told the sultan,
and as the sultan discovered, dawn after dawn
when he had heard another story
and still neither of them had died,
the question is why, when we are here
can we not love enough
not to let go?

**How many times, King Midas,**
have I considered your suffering:
no doubt, and so alone, you are misunderstood.
Why *not* reveal the intrinsic value of a leaf
by turning it to gold?

It was a mistake, though, to neglect the leaf's pathos
and still its photosynthesis
and the consciousness of the girl reaching for an apple.
The moment she brought it to her lips,
you arrested it with a fingertip:
now she has an apple to sell
but she remains hungry—did you think of that?

And then
you touched her cheek,
her breasts, the flower into which
you wished to plunge yourself—
with the best intentions I'm sure—but
look at the result—
now someone—not you, you would never—
will decide she can be *sold*.

What a pity you did not write a poem instead.
Everyone knows a poem has no intrinsic worth:
its words are like a river,
its form like the river's clay banks,
the clay made of slowly deposited repositories of plants,

tiny fish, minutely calcified insects, the decay
of multi-celled organisms
which without thought of profit
make the evolution of creatures like you possible.

Examine yourself, King Midas,
and the river freshening its hold on the planet:

when you looked at the girl, her eyes distant,
was that when the idea came
to destroy?
Now you know what you are,
and we know, too, stop it, stop it
just stop it.

# Nebuchadnezzar

Love is not love which finds a friend
grazing in a field and does not say:
Where is your coat, you must have a coat,
where is the man who took your coat?
Love is not love which observes a head lift
slowly from the grass and does not say:
I know this face with my fingers,
I have stroked this neck.
Love is not love which sees a mouth
full of hay and does not insist:
Where are your plate and cup,
where is all you gave?
Love is not love which finds a sway
of hair, like feathers and fur, and does not exclaim:
Those ears, those beautiful ears! That dazzling tail!
Love is not love which discovers a paw
or a talon amidst a display of hands and feet,
loose in the land like a cast off,
like a coat and a cup and a hat and spoon,
a body pale with rain,
and does not say: We were young together,
and now I am nearer than ever
to your beautiful mind.

# Naming the Animals in the Time of the Reptiles

Do not blame the reptile that thinks it is an
hippopotamus any more than you would chastise

the tree that believes it's a swan:
their consciousness is not your problem.

Yours is to remember
that shadows are lengthening;

and when it is the reptiles' regular time to eat,
do not mistake their attraction for love.

Look at them closely: their ridged skins shine
like golden armour around small red eyes.

Their minds make one mind as they criss-cross
and circle: to understand them think of flocking birds

or a pack of wolves.
It would take the smallest lizard a year to devour you,

but it would try.

We are safe, dear ones, as long as we know
the world is an experiment

in which no one is sure of the outcome.

## Colour Theory

Let us say that the blue
of heaven is brought forth

from the imagination of god
or an equivalent of god, which could be

the sum total of the force that spins
from a cast away body

that perceives not only the green forest
perimeter of the world,

but paint and wooden walls
and the comfort of couch and chair
and carpet.

This harmony

is conjured, like taste,
by the practice of centuries. Some

hope themselves a net,
and some use their hands:

and what's caught there's
a chemical
reaction—the base metal

of a body that burns to gold. Just

for a second the black sky
is seared with stars and the writing is plain.

It's a theory, I guess, that any good will come,
but I have my hand in my mother's hair,

and my father is in my arms
and against my breast—

such children as could make you believe.

Photograph by Xan Shian

Marilyn Bowering of Sooke, B.C. has received many awards for her writing (both poetry and fiction) including the Pat Lowther Award, the Dorothy Livesay Prize and several National Magazine awards. Her work has been shortlisted for the Governor General's Award and for international awards including the Dublin Impac Award, the Orange Prize, the Sony Award and the Prix Italia. She was a 2008 Fulbright Scholar at New York University and currently teaches at Vancouver Island University. Her most recent books are *Green* (poetry, with Exile Editions) and *What It Takes to Be Human* (novel).

# ACKNOWLEDGMENTS

Some of these poems have appeared in the following magazines and anthologies: *The Antigonish Review, Arc, CVII, ELQ/Exile: The Literary Quarterly, Grain, Gutter, The Malahat Review, New Quarterly, Prairie Fire, Framing the Garden* (ed. Linda Rogers), *The P.K. Page Trust Fund Reading* (ed. Dennis Reid), *Rocksalt* (ed. Mona Fertig & Harold Rhenisch), *The Warwick Review, Wildfire Anthology* (ed. Susan Musgrave), *The White Collar Book* (ed. Bruce & Carolyn Meyer).

To Michael for his love and support, to Seán Virgo for his editing, and to the hidden hands of *MM*, *DMB* and others.

In memory of Elizabeth Gorrie and P.K. Page.

*Epigraphs:*

Rumi: as found in *The Way of the Sufi*, ed. Idries Shah (Penguin, 1968), page 110.

P.K. Page: from *Kaleidoscope*, by P.K. Page, by permission of the Porcupine's Quill. Copyright © 2010, the Estate of P.K. Page.

Plato: as found in *The Republic Book VII, The Collected Dialogues of Plato*, ed. Hamilton and Cairns (Bollingen Series LXXI, Princeton University Press, 10th edition 1980), page 747.